WALKING *through the* FOG

HOLDING ON TO HOPE WHEN
YOU CAN'T SEE THE SUN

KRISTEN GUILLORY, Ph.D.

FOREWORD BY DANIELLE ANDERSON

Published by:
R. H. Publishing
3411 Preston Rd. Ste C-13-146
Frisco, TX. 75034

ISBN# 978-1-945693-03-8

Dedicated to Chase, Papa, and Jr.

TABLE OF CONTENTS

FOREWORD

My life changed forever on March 23, 2013. A series of horrifying and traumatic events ended with the news that my son didn't have a heartbeat. My one-year-old son, Chase, had died. Horror and sorrow and despair and anger and shock hit me all at once, and it was that day that I began to navigate all those emotions while trying to stand on truths that just didn't make sense. God is good. God cannot lie. God is in charge of everything.

This tragedy became the catalyst for the book you hold in your hand. It shook our entire family to the core, and my big sister, Dr. Kristen Guillory, was no exception. In the chapters to come, you will hear her experience—the journey the Lord had for her to take. It is a story of great transparency—she is brutally honest about her weaknesses, her failures, her pride, and her triumphs as well. But her heart is not to simply tell you a story. No, that's never been who she is. Since childhood, she has been about helping others. Encouraging them. Challenging them to move toward that which is good.

There is a common phrase used in and outside of our family—"getting Dr. G-ed." It's a phrase we use to describe the phenomenon that often happens when my sister talks to people. Whether in a one-on-one setting, a small group, or maybe even one of her university classrooms, Kristen has a keen discernment to know how to ask just the right series of probing questions that can push you to tears. And even if the tears don't come, she's pushed you. Maybe to a new way of looking at a situation. Perhaps even to a personal breakthrough. But ultimately you're pushed to freedom. Freedom from an unhealthy habit, or a dangerous thinking pattern, or even a toxic relationship.

Prepare yourself to get Dr. G-ed in this book.

I could take time here to tell you that my sister has a Bachelor's Degree from Texas Christian University, a Master's in Social Work and Doctorate of Social Work from the University of Texas at Arlington. I could tell you that she is a professional corporate trainer, a counselor, and personal speaker who has addressed thousands of people. I could tell you that she earned her Ph.D. at 27 years old and list her impressive clients. I could go on about her vast experience as a university professor and entrepreneur. She is the founder/co-founder of countless community, men's, women's, and girls' initiatives and expos that started with tens in attendance and eventually grew to thousands.

I hinted on just a small portion of Dr. G's resume. And I do mean small. But here is what I think is the most important for you to know, as you read this book. You will be hearing from Kristen Guillory—a woman who loves the Lord with all her heart, soul, mind, and strength, and a woman who loves her neighbor as herself. I told you before that she's not here to simply tell you a story. No, she wants to invite you on a journey. She will take her experiences and different lessons the Lord is continually teaching her, to encourage and challenge you. And she wants to do that because she has tasted and seen that the Lord is good, even in the darkest of times—and she wants that for you. She wants you to also experience the presence and faithfulness of the Lord in pain and in pleasure. Her heart wants more of His strength for you and less of your own. More of His truth, rather than your opinions. More of His life-giving-pleasures-forever-more plan, and none of your I-know-what's-best-for-me agenda.

So get your Bible, journal and pen ready. Study the scriptures she points you to for yourself. Answer her questions honestly. Take her up on lots of her challenges. And lean into the Lord— every step of the way—even if it's uncomfortable, and even if you're not sure what He's doing.

God IS good. God CANNOT lie. God IS in charge of everything. The truths that were hard for me to embrace in the midst of tragedy back in 2013 have become warm blankets to my soul, a sure and steady foundation when the bottom falls out.

Grace and peace to you on your journey.

Danielle Anderson
Little sister to Kristen, wife to Tedashii,
Mom to Jaden, Chase, Callen, and Kai

INTRODUCTION

The year 2013 changed everything—intense devastation, joy, confusion and truly realizing that the Lord is there when the bottom falls from beneath you. More than anything, I was broken most of the year. I felt lost. I felt out of control. I could have never imagined what the year would become. I hid my pain from many people. The pain didn't end in 2013 because I would struggle in different ways for the next few years. That year was the catalyst for me to be in a place where I was truly trying to trust and seek the Lord, which honestly is a place I hadn't been in the past.

For the past several years, I have been blessed to be able to speak to different groups across the country. In August of 2013 while at Wednesday night service, the Lord gave me a message that He wanted me to share at a women's conference that September. This was during a time I had nothing left and was below fumes. Because of this, I had made a decision earlier that year not to take on any more speaking engagements. So when this opportunity arose, my first thought was to decline. I asked the Lord, "God, are you sure you want me to do this?" And He said "Yes." And that message would become the basis for this book.

This message was unlike any other message I had shared. This was a message of transparency, tears, and no masks. In addition to sharing about my pain, I shared about the pain a friend was experiencing that year.

A few months prior to giving the message I spoke to this friend who had suddenly lost his father, which devastated him. He explained his faith walk to me by sharing that he felt as if he was walking through the fog, not able to see in front of him but knew God was holding his hand. I had no clue that I would be applying the same description to my journey.

Through everything I encountered, I was reminded of 2 Corinthians 12:9, "My grace is sufficient for you, for my power is made perfect in weakness." What a powerful verse. I definitely felt weak most of the year and years thereafter. To know that God's power is perfect in our weakness is amazing news.

Although it might be difficult and even impossible, it's important that we try to seek Him, trust Him, and be real with Him and ourselves. We have to be honest with ourselves and honest with God. We have to stop hiding things. We may be in pain and that pain might last for a while. Good news, The Lord knows and He can and wants to comfort us. But I didn't truly know this in the previous years.

Most of the years prior to 2013 were fairly smooth. In 2012, I celebrated a new nephew, a new relationship, a great job, met a weight loss goal, and I traveled to many places, including the Dominican Republic! Life was great—I got comfortable.

I was comfortable ... too comfortable. And being comfortable is not always a good place because, for me, when I am comfortable, I lean on myself, only. I forgot to pray, I forgot to just say, "Thank you," and I forgot that I needed the Lord. During that time my prayers were very shallow. I didn't need Him. But when things are really hard, I discovered that He is there the whole time; I had just turned my back on Him.

2012 was a Good year, but not a God year. 2013 was a God year. 2013 had already started off quite strange. I really didn't know what was going on. Let me paint the picture. I was uncomfortable. On Martin Luther King Jr. Day, I woke up very uncomfortable. Uncomfortable about the relationship I was in. I'm the analytical type. So, I pulled out my laptop and began to conduct, what the business world calls a "S.W.O.T." analysis on the gentleman I was seeing. What is a S.W.O.T. analysis? It is one's Strengths, Weaknesses, Opportunities, and Threats. I began to analyze him through this lens. Crazy, right? I worked through all these questions only to discover that this process wasn't working.

The next month, things got worse. The gentleman and I broke up. This was my first break up. I'm thinking, "Wait a minute. Why did I get in my first relationship in my thirties for it to end? What?" I didn't understand the meaning of this, even though my family and friends called it the best break up in the world. Why did they feel that way? There was respect. We paid each other compliments, there was encouragement, and there were laughs.

God used that situation to show me so much about me—not about him.

This is where the story really begins. I had no clue of the journey the Lord would take me on over the next few years. I can tell you that I am not the same person I was prior to 2013. The things God showed me about myself were things I needed to know and understand, and honestly, it hurt.

I invite you to come on this journey. A journey of confusion, hurt, joy, frustration, brokenness and the Lord.

You have this book in your hands because you feel as though you are walking through the fog. You might feel like giving up, you might be suffering, you might be broken, you might be exhausted, you might be experiencing secondary trauma, and you might be experiencing first hand trauma.

Please know the Lord can handle all of it. As my sister shared earlier, "God is good. God cannot lie. God is in charge of everything." How powerful is this? My sister, whose precious son went to be with the Lord, still believes this to her core. Now, are you a bad person if you don't quite believe that, yet? No, you are not.

I am so thankful that you picked up this book. This tells me that you need help, that you're not done, that you don't know what to do. You can't see the next step. But I know Who can see it, and will be with you.

In some of the chapters there will be Scriptures or passages. I pray that you would take some time to read and reflect on the words and do a study on the passages. I pray these Words will encourage you as you read them. I encourage you to pray before you read each chapter, so that the Lord will show you anything He needs to reveal to you. I want to encourage you to pray and jot down your thoughts.

Each chapter will also come with questions for a closer examination of your own thoughts. While this book is a resource to walking through the fog, the Bible is the true source. So please have your Bible handy while reading this book. The only true comfort, revelation, healing or direction is through the Lord and His Word.

In chapters 1-5, I share my story that includes my painful truth. Chapter 6 starts the steps for you to take while you're walking this journey. Throughout each of the chapters are questions and challenges for you.

Thank you for letting me share my story with you. Please know that I don't mean to imply that my story is worse than anything you may be going through or that this book is only for those who have experienced the loss of a loved one.

You know why you need this book. This is your journey. My prayer is that you will not only be challenged as you read and work through some of the areas that relate to your own life, but you will also see the power of God and what He will do, if you let Him.

Chapter 1

I HAD NO CLUE

In 2011, I had no clue that the next year would be one of the best years of my life, or so I thought.

I had no clue I was going to reach a weight loss goal, get into my first relationship and travel as much as I did.

I had no clue that I would become an aunt to a second nephew.

In 2011, I had no clue that in 2013 I would look back on 2012 and recognize that it was a good year, but it wasn't a God year.

I had no clue that that relationship would end at the beginning of 2013.

I had no clue that my second nephew would go to be with the Lord, nine days after he turned just one-year-old.

I had no clue I would be in as much pain as I was.

I had no clue how much my nephew's death would impact me.

I had no clue that I wouldn't be able to be the fixer.

I had no clue that I would be broken. I had no clue that later that year I would be below fumes.

WALKING THROUGH THE FOG

In 2011, I had no clue that I was wearing a mask that would be removed in 2013.

I had no clue that in 2013 I would be offered an awesome tenure track position just shortly after losing my nephew.

I had no clue that I would later live in two cities because of this job.

I had no clue that a year later I would be led to leave that very job.

I had no clue that a few months later my grandfather would die.

In 2011, I had no clue that in the years to come I would no longer be friends with four women who were very important to me, which pained me more than many know.

I had no clue that I would see the Lord in ways I had never seen Him.

I had no clue that leaving my professor's position wasn't about pursuing projects and work, but that the Lord wanted me to get closer to Him.

I had no clue that six months after leaving my job, I would receive the largest contract I had ever received.

I had no clue that two months later that contract would be taken away. I was devastated.

I had no clue that three months later, my uncle would pass away.

I had no clue that I would struggle financially for the first time in my life.

I had no clue that I would battle depression—twice (at the end of 2013 and at the end of 2015) and go to counseling.

I had no clue that in December 2016, I would have emergency surgery to remove a tumor and one of my ovaries.

I had no clue that my sister would give birth to two more sons. Callen was born in December of 2013. His birth would provide more joy than we could have imagined. And the awesome Kai would bless us with his presence in August of 2015.

I had no clue that although Callen and Kai would never physically meet Chase, they would know and recognize their older brother.

In 2011, I had no clue that in the years to come I would truly see the Lord in ways I had never seen Him.

I had no clue that I would truly want to seek His face.

I had no clue that I would discover joy and peace.

Literally, I had no clue ...

CHALLENGE

I wonder if you can relate to anything I've shared. Underline, highlight or put a checkmark by the things we have in common. Are there any things you marked that you've tried to keep a secret? Did you think you were the only one? Do you realize you are not alone?

"So now I am glad to boast about my weaknesses, so that the power of Christ can work. But he said to me, 'My grace is sufficient for you, for my power is made perfect in weakness.' Therefore, I will boast all the more gladly about my weaknesses" (2 Corinthians 12:9).

This scripture was often a go-to scripture for me during the difficult times. There were many times I felt weak, and it was only God's perfect power that would carry me.

What is grace?

_____
_____
_____
_____
_____

What does sufficient mean?

_____
_____
_____
_____
_____

What does perfect mean?

_____

_____

_____

_____

_____

What are your "I HAD NO CLUE" moments?

I had no clue ...

_____

_____

_____

_____

_____

_____

_____

_____

_____

_____

_____

_____

_____

_____

_____

WALKING THROUGH THE FOG

Chapter 2

THE DAY THAT CHANGED IT ALL

As previously mentioned, I went through my first break up in 2013; it was mid-February to be exact. I was so confused— why I would get into my first relationship at 32 for it to end? Shortly after thinking this, God said, "I've called you to work with women and men, but you weren't empathetic in the area of break-ups." This was true. If someone broke up, I gave them the cliché advice, "Oh, you'll find somebody better. You can move on." But I realized that in that season, that advice doesn't help.

A week after we broke up, I was helping two women heal after a breakup. Throughout the rest of the year, I helped about 50 individuals and have since written an article called "Dr. G's Break Up Tips" that's been featured many different places.

There was one thing that was unique about this breakup. It was a "good breakup," according to family and friends because there was mutual respect, compliments, and laughter during the break-up chat. Although it was a good breakup it was still a break up, which means there was a break. I didn't admit to anyone that I was hurt, sad, and needed healing. I remember thinking; "If this is what a good break up feels like, what must a bad one feel like?" I also thought "Why do people go from one relationship to the next? Is the reason to avoid dealing with the pain? Is it to pretend? Often people will say "Move on, you can find better." There's a problem with the phrase. You might have actually thought you were with better, and there is no need to move on because you need to pause and be still with the Lord.

Those first few weeks were hard. I went to Houston to visit my dad for spring break in order to get away. When I came back, I was energized and ready to go. The week after spring break was a pretty good week.

Friday of that week, (March 22), as I was driving to Denton, Texas, to visit my nephews, I was on the phone talking to a very close friend who had suddenly lost his father. He said, "I'm not good. I'm fractured, but I'm functional." I was encouraged by him and his faith. He said, "I am in the valley, but my spirit is strong." Wow! I could not believe that he was still trusting the Lord after his father, one of his closest friends, passed away. I was in awe of his faith.

I then arrived in Denton and went to see my sister and my nephews, Jaden and Chase—ages three and one. I shared with my sister that I had a speaking engagement the next day where I would be talking to individuals who were completing a Work Force program. I mentioned that I was going encourage them and share "You may be fractured, but you're functional." The real reason I went to visit my sister and nephews was because Chase, the one-year-old, was sick. I just wanted to see him. I could see that he was ill, but he seemed to be getting better. Because of the speaking engagement, I had to leave earlier than normal.

March 23rd is the day my life changed.

After that speaking engagement, which was amazing, I checked my phone, saw an alarming text message from my mom, and immediately called her. "Mom, what's going on?" My mom then said two words: "Chase passed."

Upon hearing this news, I fell to the ground and began to wail. I remember lying on the ground, crying and repeatedly yelling the word "What?" My precious one-year and nine-day-old nephew had passed away.

I don't have children, and I feel like my nephews are like my own children in a way. Those who have attended my trainings or classes know that I often talk about my nephews.

This was the first time in my life that something brought me to my knees, literally. "I'm sorry, what did you say?" That's all I kept saying, "What?" After maybe 10 minutes of being on the floor, I got up, called my dad and told him the horrible news. I have maybe seen my dad cry once, and to hear his heartbreak over the phone was devastatingly heartbreaking.

I was in tears. I was shaking. "I can't believe this. It's a baby. This beautiful baby!" I began to think about my sister. "Oh my God this is my sister's son. Oh my God, this is my brother-in-law's son. Oh my God, this is my mom's grandbaby." My next thought was, "I have to leave and get to my sister's house." The staff at the venue would not allow me to drive. They insisted, and I am so glad they did. One of the amazing women drove me to my aunt's house and from there we headed to Denton.

The next two weeks were just God. The fog was the thickest it has ever been in my life. When my aunt, uncle and I arrived at my sister and brother-in-law's house, there was heartbreak all around. I didn't know what to do. As the oldest, I wanted to fix things. I am a fixer. I'm supposed to fix it. People came to me for answers, and I always had them. That is, except for this day. I had no answer. This was literally the first time I had no solution, no suggestion, and no remedy.

I mentioned that I describe those two weeks and beyond as 'Just God.' Here's why. There is no way that my sister, brother in law, my nephew Jaden, I or anyone else could have made it through without the Lord. I cannot imagine the pain my sister was in. My pain was horrible. In the midst, believe it or not, there actually were some smiles and some laughter in that household. Not that anybody was in denial, because trust me, there was heartache and heartbreak. We were like, "Okay God, carry us because 'us' can't do anything." The Lord provided so much comfort for my sister, my brother-in-law and Jaden. It was beautiful. The Lord provided support for me through my friends.

As the oldest sibling, I felt like I had to protect everybody. I had to look after everybody. I have to protect everyone, so I went into protector mode. I may not have a solution, but I can protect. I can help.

I thought, "Let me put my grief on the side for my family—My sister. My nephew. My brother-in-law. My mom. My aunt. My family." The day that my nephew passed away, I told a close friend, "I have to be strong for my family." I was unaware that she shared this with her friend who is a pastor. This pastor sent me a text message that helped me more than he will ever know. The text said, *"You don't have to be strong for anyone; let God do that for you. Trying not to grieve is like trying not to sweat. You must let it happen."* Those words allowed me to breathe just a bit. I later came to realize our strength alone on our best day doesn't even get us by. So how dare I even think that I am strong enough to help somebody else when I don't have any strength? And I definitely needed the Lord's strength for what was to come.

I will always remember something a friend said during

that first week. "The Tiki who was here yesterday is gone. You will be entering a new normal." That was hard to hear at first but he was correct. I have often heard people say things like "I'm going to get back to the old me." But there is a problem with that. The "old me" had your loved one or the thing you no longer have. So there is no way to get back to the "old me." And that is ok. For those of you grieving, please remember this.

I have an extensive background in mental health but all of my education didn't prepare me for what I was going through. I truly was carried by the Lord. I helped plan the service for Chase. I helped pick out the flowers, something I would have never thought I would do. I slept at my sister's house that week. I was almost a zombie because I was in work mode. And because Chase wasn't my child, I figured all of the attention needed to go to my sister and brother-in-law. Although I had friends checking on me, I felt invisible and alone during that time. No one checks on the aunt, right? I got used to that. One day in particular, I was working on the obituary when one of my sister's friends saw me and suggested that I get out of the house because he knew that I hadn't left. That encouragement was needed. So I left the house for a while. I checked my many voicemails of people expressing their condolences. I decided to call some people back. The first was a call to one of my former youth. I was beyond drained at this point and didn't feel like chatting. When he got on the phone he said, "I was just calling to say I love you." This moved me to tears and was what I needed to hear in that exact moment. Later, I realized that I didn't need to try to hide my pain. Yes, the aunt has pain. Yes, people do check on the aunt.

When I arrived back at the house, my sister asked me if I would like to share some words at Chase's service. And I obviously said, "Yes." This opportunity was more important to me, than any other time I was asked to share. I wasn't sharing as Dr. G, I was sharing as Tiki (my family nickname), Chase's aunt.

The day of the service was, as you can imagine, truly difficult. This was the second hardest day of our family's life. My sister was weak. I was so sad, and I wanted to take away her pain. I wanted to offer some words to my brother-in-law but I didn't have them.

The service was beautiful. There was praise and worship, smiles, tears, and talk of the goodness of the Lord. My sister and brother-in-law actually got up and shared in front of everyone. They wanted to make sure to point everyone to the Lord.

There was a beautiful slideshow that played, and right after, it was my turn to share. As I walked up to the podium, I had no clue how I was going to get through my words. I got there and looked out at everyone. No words came out of my mouth. I was on the verge of breaking down when my dad came up to comfort me. I said to him, "Don't touch me," which apparently added a little humor and cut the tension. Here is a little bit of what I shared at the service:

"Chase, so beautiful and such a sweet spirit lived a life here on Earth that was full of love, fun, joy, music, dancing and travel, along with so many aunts and uncles.

"Our lives are forever changed for the better by the blessing of Chase. And we will continue to be blessed by him. I thank God for allowing Tedashii to find my sister as one of the many blessings of that union is Chase and Jaden. These two are amazing parents, and you can see this through the joy of their children.

"To my sister and brother-in-law—I love you; we love you, and I am encouraged by your faith and hope in the Lord Jesus Christ. God's strength through you is amazing. We are here for you. God has a plan, and His plans aren't always ours—often we don't understand His plans, but we trust Him. There are many emotions from sadness and confusion, but we must trust Him. There were smiles and laughter this week. There is Joy we find in the Lord.

"When we are suffering, we need comforting. God is the God of ALL comfort in ANY affliction. One job of the Holy Spirit is to be a Comforter ... to come alongside and help. Our vertical relationship with God is experienced in our horizontal relationships with one another. He uses the family of God to comfort the family of God. That's why we need to be connected to the Body of Christ. When we go through the fire, God is with us. We must develop a God-focus during our affliction. God has a ministry in our pain."

My nephew has shaped my faith. At a new faculty orientation later that year, someone said, "Write down the names of the people who have shaped your faith." I wrote two names. Chase was one of those names. My one-year-old nephew has immensely impacted my faith. My nephew led a life that we only dream of; it was one of happiness, laughter, dancing and love. He didn't know this horrible world, and he's where we want to be. Just an amazing life!

After the service, I took off another week from work to try and help my sister, my brother-in-law and my 3-year-old nephew, who missed and still misses his brother. (Don't ever underestimate age. He misses his brother.)

Once I returned to campus, my students said, "Dr. G, we didn't know if you were coming back." How could they know? I didn't know. What I did know was the Lord was still carrying me and that He told me to share what happened over the last few weeks with my students. At that point in my life, I was rarely transparent in class and I am so thankful that I was obedient and shared. I cried. I was honest, and I talked about the Lord. I had so many students share with me about a loss they had and more. I was able to give some of them permission to still grieve a loved one.

Since I was still grieving as well, it took so much energy for me to teach. There were days when I arrived home from work so exhausted, and I'd just lie down on the couch for the rest of the evening. There were also days I didn't feel like teaching, yet I continued. I know there were days the Lord told me to be still, but I didn't listen to Him. I am sure that the Lord told me to stop trying to handle everyone's stuff, but I ignored Him. I didn't take any time off for me. The time I did take off was to help plan the service and support my family.

The previous year, I had been working on my physical health—in the gym at least four times a week. During that time, I didn't have the energy to go to the gym.

I pushed my grief to the side. Yet, in the midst of this truly difficult time something quite astonishing happened. I learned that I believed what I had always said about God. I learned that He absolutely gives us what we need, when we need it, and so much more. I just had to trust and be willing to get in the back seat and allow the Lord to drive. At times, I just needed to trust and get in the trunk. Why? Because sometimes when I get a little peek of something to come, I start putting my own logic on it. I was in the driver's seat far too long.

That semester ended well. However, it took a lot out of me. Then to my surprise, I received a job offer for a professor position on at another university. I wasn't looking for another job, and I wasn't interested in this one.

A few months before my nephew's passing, a university began recruiting me. They first contacted me in the Fall of 2012, but I wasn't interested. They followed up in January, and I still wasn't interested.

I thought, "The salary is too low. Nope, not going to happen, and I'm not moving." I had a conversation with the university and shared my concerns about moving. Their response was, "That's okay. You can commute."

I continued with, "Well, your salary is too low."

They said, "That's okay; the Dean will change it."

"So, can I talk about Jesus in the classroom?"

"Yep!"

"Oh. I can play hip hop?

"Yep!"

Oh, I didn't want it. Why did this job come at this time? "I don't want to move. I'm cool where I am," I thought.

This is exactly the reason it was time to move. I was comfortable where I was. When I am comfortable, I rely on myself and not the Lord.

If I am going to be completely honest, I wasn't interested in this new position because the university was in West Texas—a place I never wanted to live.

To my amazement I accepted the job offer. I was truly seeking the Lord. I thought, "Lord, why would I get a job two and a half hours away now? During this season?"

The Lord said, "Go," so I accepted the job not knowing why but knowing I was still broken.

WALKING THROUGH THE FOG

Can you relate to me in any way? If so, how?

_____

_____

_____

_____

_____

What are you grieving? Or what should you grieve?

_____

_____

_____

_____

_____

Why are you walking through the fog?

_____

_____

_____

_____

_____

If you had to give your life a title for what it is right now, what would it be?

_____

_____

_____

_____

_____

What would you hope your 'life title' to be in the near future?

_____

_____

_____

_____

_____

The following are the lyrics to the song "Chase" by his dad
Tedashii

I will go chasing you
Trusting you
Hope in you
Forever, forever, oh

When I first held you I cried
If I would have known a year later I wouldn't have you in this
life
I would've never let you go, just held you close
One of the few things that really mattered to me most
Seems unfair how life treats us down here
We grow attached to the very people that can disappear
I would do anything to have you back again
One more smile, just one more kiss
To hear you cry when you don't get your way
I never knew to cherish that and now it seems too late
At least it feels that way, how I'll never forget
How I'll keep holding on until I see you again

You give, and you take,

WALKING THROUGH THE FOG

Through it all I will chase after your heart
Not your head,
When my heart don't understand

I will go chasing you
Trusting you
Hope in you
Forever, forever, oh
In the morning I would play with you
Your smile would be the only thing to help me make it
through
So many things I want to say to you
But I guess that Heaven couldn't wait for you
I dreamed of a life that would last past mine
Now when I wake up I wish that I could stop time
He gives and takes away, what more can I say?
I just trust and hope that he'll make everything ok
I know there's never been a day that he didn't love me
Even now it's hard to see, but he's there above me
And every time I think about it I know your with him
So I keep holding on until I see you again
You give, and you take,
Through it all I will chase after your heart
Not your head,
When my heart don't understand

I will go chasing you
Trusting you
Hope in you
Forever, forever, oh

Chapter 3

BELOW FUMES

Once the semester ended in May of 2013, I needed a moment to be still and cut off from the world. For my birthday (May 24) that year, I decided to take a staycation. Staycation means a vacation in your house (or your city). I turned off my phone for a few days. I hadn't turned off my phone, on purpose, in years.

During my staycation, I decided to clean my room. As I'm cleaning my room, God said, "You know, you're really like your house. Your exterior is presentable, but at the core of your house is your room, and your room is a mess. At the core of you, you're a mess." He had my attention. I dropped any and all distractions.

Little did I know that the staycation was the start of a painful pruning season. This is when God began to show me how ugly I was. He began to show me my flaws ... and it hurt. And I was still hurt and grieving.

Later that summer, I had a two-day speaking engagement scheduled. Unfortunately, I had nothing else to give—or fortunately, depending on how you look at it—God had to carry me. After the engagement, I knew I wasn't good. One of my students joined me and on the ride home said "Dr. G the talk was amazing but you seem really sad." I was. I didn't realize how sad I was, and I didn't realize others could tell because I was the queen of wearing masks. I was also pushing it too much, and to be honest, I hadn't been good in a long time. So I began to look up lake houses for rent and booked one.

I packed up and headed off to a solo, four-day retreat. I was tapped out. I was below fumes. I wasn't good at all. Anyone who knows me, knows that if you hear me say, "I'm tapped out," something is wrong. I had only been tapped out one other time in my life. But this was the first time I had ever said it out loud to another person.

I arrived to a beautiful location, took in my luggage, played some music, and within 10 minutes I was in tears. The words of a song by gospel artist J Moss penetrated my heart. It's a song I had heard many times before, but this time was different. The words are:

"Forgive me, Oh Lord, It's me again. I've disobeyed Your word, I've slipped out of Your will. Regretful, I stand - me again."

Through my tears, I started to apologize. And this is when my "How Dare I" moments started.

Describe your sadness, your pain, your confusion.

_____
_____
_____
_____
_____

Do you need to schedule a staycation? After something devastating, it is a good idea to consider going out of town or taking a staycation outside of your home. It could literally be 12 hours. What is the first step you need to take to get your staycation going?

_____
_____
_____
_____
_____

What if I were to challenge you to turn off your phone for a few days? For even one day? For one hour? How might you feel? It's amazing how attached we are to our phones.

_____
_____
_____
_____
_____

ACTION:

I challenge you to pick a day and time to turn off your phone for a minimum of an hour. (Sleeping doesn't count). During that time, you can pray, nap, watch TV. Just take a moment to unplug.

WHAT DAY? _____ WHAT TIME?_____

(For more information, visit kristenguillory.com to locate the Blog-Staycation Kit for tips.)

Chapter 4

"HOW DARE I"

The following is from my journal entries while I was staying at the lake for this retreat.

I need to trust and love God with all of my heart and mind. Really, do I even know what that means? As often as I want to brag about Jaden (my oldest nephew), how often do I do this about God?

- *How dare I try to limit Him and focus on such small things.*

- *How dare I only go to Him when I am only in need or in pain.*

- *How dare I forget what He did and is doing for me. He sent His son to die a brutal death for me, whose life is but a vapor.*

- *How dare I think I am more important than I am?*

- *Wow!*

- *How dare I think I am in control at all. He knew me before I was born.*

- *How dare I be short or rude to family members.*

- *How dare I put too much thought on things that don't deserve it.*

- *How dare I not use and fully cultivate my gifts.*

- *How dare I ever try to make things about me. It's not about me! It's about God and His love and Him using me for His glory. I must make a daily/hourly effort to keep my focus on Him and not worry and stress.*

- *How dare I ever worry or stress.*

- *How dare I think I can fix things. How flawed I am and how flawed has my thinking been because I wasn't thinking with a Kingdom perspective.*

- *How dare I ever put myself on a pedestal.*

- *How dare I be selfish.*

- *How dare I not thank You.*

- *How dare I forget that You created everything.*

- *How dare I put a guy on the pedestal.*

- *How dare I not ask for help.*

- *How dare I not forgive.*

- *How dare I cancel on my nephews to hang out with friends or the guy I was dating.*

- *How dare I forget that I am not in control.*

- *How dare I let pride rule.*

- *How dare I not take time to pray.*

This went on for a while. I kept saying, "Lord, I'm sorry." I repented. I cried. I was pruned. All was necessary. I also continued grieving. I had compounded grief. The break up that I had put aside, after the loss of my nephew, but then I put the grief of my nephew on the side to help my family. Then, I didn't grieve my old job. I didn't stop. It all just snowballed, to the point where I broke. During this lake retreat, I got a chance to continue or at least start to grieve each of these things. I got a chance to be honest with the Lord.

I began to thank the Lord. I told Him that I wanted to trust Him. "I can say this because You've given me so much, and Your grace is more sufficient than I even understand."

It was exhausting and necessary. During my time there, I realized how hurt I was. I cried each day. In the past, I prided myself for not crying, and even would call myself a "G." Tears are okay and needed. I heard someone say that tears are sometimes those prayers we don't know how to put into words.

I wonder if you can relate to anything I wrote in my journal during that time. I still slip back to some of those "How Dare I's." Isn't it amazing how easy it is to fall into these old patterns and thoughts? Isn't it amazing how powerful life becomes when we keep our focus on the Lord?

Now it's your turn.

WHAT ARE YOUR "HOW DARE I'S?"

How Dare I_____

How Dare I_____

How Dare I_____

How Dare I_____

How Dare I_____

How Dare I_____

How Dare I_____

How Dare I_____

How Dare I_____

How Dare I_____

How Dare I_____

Three weeks after that solo retreat I began to clean out my campus office in preparation for my new professor position in West Texas. One day, as I was driving to what was to become my former campus, I was jammin' to the radio. All of a sudden I said, "This will be my last year of full-time teaching." After I said that, I turned up the radio and tried to ignore what I had said because that didn't make any sense ... AT ALL!

WALKING THROUGH THE FOG

Chapter 5

STEPPING OUT IN FAITH

I truly didn't understand why the Lord would have me go to this new university at this time in particular. But I knew He told me to go. So I did.

I had a unique arrangement. I lived in West Texas three days per week and Dallas the other days. I truly loved my time in West Texas and at the university. As the school year was ending, I was told I was going to be given an apartment during the next school year. I was also invited to be on many boards and committees on the campus. I was also known around this West Texas town, even outside of the university. I thought I was gearing up for year number two.

Two weeks after the semester ended, my best friend and I went on a short getaway. Both mornings, while sitting on the balcony, the Lord nudged me to leave that awesome position as a professor. YES, the same position I had for one year that I initially didn't even want.

The following is an excerpt from a blog post where I shared about that journey of leaving my job.

"May of 2014 I felt God beginning to tell me that it was time to step away from my amazing professor position with an amazing university. What??? Who does that?? He said that it was time to fully walk in my purpose. I ignored Him because that was crazy. I loved being with

my students and encouraging them. I had just taken the job out of obedience the year before, and 2013 was the most devastating and the most difficult year of my life.

"I was like, "Lord, can I just stay?" I told God … yes, you read that correctly, "I told God" that I would give it until mid-July to make the decision, but only if I had some financial gigs lined up. I went back and forth all summer weighing my options. God used so many ways to tell me that it was time, but I still didn't listen. I like stability and being comfortable. This would be very uncomfortable. Leaving a job was not supposed to have been a part of my story. I was bragging about my best friend who left her job, saying that she was walking in PLATINUM FAITH. I was happy to brag about her journey, but I didn't want that journey.

"So, in early July of that year (2014), I went to Kids Across America (KAA) with my sister and her family. She asked me to do something with her called Tree Tops. At first, I said, "No," and then I decided to join her. The rule was once you place your foot on the log you can't turn around. So we started to go up the log—(We were holding each other's shoulders)—and about 25 steps up, I regretted making this decision. I wanted to turn around—FOR REAL!

"We finally made it to the top, and I said, 'I'll be the first to quit; I don't want to do this.' I was terrified. I mean terrified.

"My sister said, 'I have never seen you like this.'

"I have a fear of heights and we were walking on a wire that was 35 feet in the air! Yes, 35 FEET! There were about 15 stations/components to this.

"By the time we got to the 8th or 9th station, my sister asked me, 'Are you afraid of falling?'

"My response was, 'Uhh, yes!'

"She said, 'If you fall, you aren't going anywhere.' Why? Because we were in harnesses.

"So, I decided to fall (after sitting for a while) and let the harness hold me. She was right, I didn't go anywhere. Toward the end of the tree top experience, I fell and got up. Then I began to feel weak and someone had to come and help me. We finished, and I was so happy to be done and that I did it!

"Later that night, God used that experience to show me what it would be like once I leave my job. He showed me that I will be scared. I will want to turn around. I will need support. I will fall, but as with the tree tops experience, I was in the harness the entire time. I wasn't going anywhere. God said the harness represents Me. I will have you the entire time, but remember, you have to rely on, trust Me and remember that I'm there.

"The next day I made the decision to leave my job. So in July of 2014, I left my amazing professor job, which HANDS DOWN WAS THE BIGGEST STEP IN FAITH I HAD EVER TAKEN ... STILL IS.

"This journey has been just like the tree tops experience. There have been times when I wanted to turn around, times I thought that I made the wrong decision. I have been scared. I've been afraid to really show and use my gifts. I've been afraid to post videos and articles. I have dealt with fear and doubt. I have been confused. I have had to rely on my amazing support system. I have relied on God.

"God has been with me the entire time, and He has provided in amazing ways! Some amazing things have happened, amazing opportunities and connections! Doors have been opened. Doors have been closed. I've said, "No" to some things. I've felt so vulnerable. I've also seen God in ways I've never seen Him. I have been so UNCOMFORTABLE. I'm so thankful for all of it! And so excited about so much! The journey continues! Some have not fully understood. They thought I made a mistake which is okay ... because I have thought the same thing at times." July 2015

What is interesting is that when I shared this via social media I started it off by saying that the Lord told me it's time to pursue my purpose. Actually, what the Lord said was that it was time. I knew He meant it's time to leave. At that time, I didn't know why, but I assumed it was to pursue projects. What I didn't know was that the Lord would reveal the true reason for me leaving my job, just one month after I shared that post.

One month later, I was in the Dominican Republic. An acquaintance was going to visit her family in the Dominican Republic that summer and invited me to join her. Since my funds were tight, I didn't think I would even be taking a vacation. God, however, provided through her and her family to make it a memorable visit.

This acquaintance called to inform me that there would not be enough room for me to join her but offer the use of the family apartment at another time during the summer. I asked her how much I should pay her family. She told me not worry about it. I persisted. She then said something I will never forget. "Accept the blessing Dr. G." I was blown away. How much more could God do?

Most of my airfare was paid for with my miles earned from a credit card. My lodging was provided for by her family, as well as my meals. Wow! One day while there, her family and I went to the beach. I got in the ocean and was enjoying looking at the palm trees and water when I heard the Lord say, "While you are so busy pursuing your purpose, make sure you are pursuing Me." The Lord hadn't led me to leave my job to start other work. He led me to leave in order to start working on my relationship with Him.

That hit me like a ton of bricks. And from that point, I began to try to pursue the Lord and not projects. Now, have I followed this the entire time? No. There were times when I was sliding a bit back to pursuing projects. And when this happened, the Lord intervened to stop me. And stop me is what He did in December of 2016.

I woke up on December 17th to head to a brunch with some college friends. An hour after arriving, I began to experience some pain. I thought the pain was related to something I ate. When we arrived to my friend's home, I went to the restroom and wound up lying down on the floor. My friends didn't know this is what I was doing. I finally left and headed to my car. They did try to get me to stay in order to rest but I just wanted to be in my own space. By the time I made it to my car, I was in so much pain, I had to lay on my back seat. After about 30 minutes I called my friend who was hosting the brunch, and she rushed me to the hospital. I was moaning in pain on the way there.

Upon arrival, I was still moaning in pain. They put me in a wheelchair and rushed me to the back. A doctor saw me and told the nurses to hurry and get me a room.

My pain was a level 10 for about six hours. I had never experienced that level of physical pain. To help with the pain, I was given two doses of morphine, which did nothing for the pain. I was then given a third dose and my pain was now at a 9. I would later learn that I had a large, non-cancerous tumor that was twisting one of my ovaries. I did not expect to hear this. I was then told that I would have to have emergency surgery to remove both. Hearing this overwhelmed me. The doctor asked me if I was scared. I said no. It was just a lot to take in.

The surgery went well, praise God. Because of the size of the tumor, the doctors had to perform a C-Section to remove it. In addition to the C-Section, they made three other incisions on my stomach which would later cause additional pain during recovery. My family stayed in the waiting room all night. The doctors told me that I had to take it easy and not work out for six to nine weeks. I couldn't even wear my beloved heels.

I would then be in recovery for seven weeks. I spent a month at my mother's home. I am so thankful for her and my brother's care. I was in so much pain. It hurt to walk. It hurt to sneeze. It hurt to laugh. It hurt to cough. It hurt to move. I wasn't able to fully stand up straight for about 11 days.

I entered 2017 not really being able to walk. This was not the plan. I was so confused—starting another significant walking through the fog moment. The Lord would lead me to use this time to reflect. I took time to surrender everything I was doing to the Lord and truly ask Him if I should be doing certain things. I also watched about 30 movies.

The first week, I was in a lot of pain.

Then, by the second week, I was confused, frustrated, and struggled with some not-great thoughts.

By the third week, I finally surrendered and got out of

the driver's seat. I realized I couldn't rush the healing, but I could slow it down. I realized that this happened for a reason.

Without stopping for those weeks, I would have continued doing things that the Lord hadn't cleared. I would have launched things the Lord hadn't cleared. I would not be where I am now. I took time to reflect on the last year and saw how much the Lord had done. I realized that 80 percent of my speaking and training engagements did not come from my efforts. The Lord had provided them.

Through all of these journeys—my nephew, leaving jobs, the 4-day lake retreat, the Dominican Republic, and surgery, I have learned some hard lessons. I've learned how to walk through the fog, especially when there are hard moments. Now, I am still learning and growing. I forget to pray and stop at times … but it's MUCH better.

I'm, now, going to offer you seven steps to take while you're walking through the fog times in your life. Please take time to truly sit in each question and honestly answer. Take time to read and re-read the scriptures and even sit in the scriptures. So, what does "sit in" mean? Take your time, ponder, and reflect. And final encouragement- consider reading one step per day or even per week.

Are you ready?

ACTION:

Please take time to pray before you read the next chapter. Pray about what you need.

WALKING THROUGH THE FOG

Take a few moments to write down some things you have gone through in the past that you didn't think you would make it through. And after you write them take a few moments to reflect and thank the Lord for seeing you through.

_____

_____

_____

_____

_____

_____

_____

_____

_____

_____

_____

_____

_____

_____

_____

_____

_____

_____

_____

_____

_____

_____

_____

_____

_____

_____

_____

Chapter 6

STEP 1: BREATHE AND BE STILL

"Be still and know that I am God"
(Psalm 46:10).

What does being still mean to you?

_____

_____

_____

_____

_____

Describe the last time you were truly still.

_____

_____

_____

_____

_____

If you haven't been still, describe the reason why.

_____

_____

_____

_____

_____

"And he said unto them, The Sabbath was made for man, and not man for Sabbath" (Mark 2:27-28)

"My soul finds rest in God alone, my salvation comes from him. He alone is my rock and my salvation, He is my fortress. I will never be shaken"
(Psalm 62:1, 2).

According to the scripture, in whom does your soul find rest?

_____

_____

_____

_____

_____

When is the last time you gave yourself permission to be still, take ten minutes for yourself and rest?

Anyone who has ever had me in class since 2011 knows that from day one I say, "It's OK to take a break." So, right now, please say out loud, "It's OK to take a break."

One more time . . . It's OK to take a break."

God dropped 'be still' on my heart the day my nephew went to be with Him. He said, "You need to be more like your nephew. If you remember, Chase was always so calm and always smiling." God said, "Be like him. Be still and look around."

Well, I was NEVER still. I was moving too much, not

just with work and ministry, but also with my social life. I was NEVER still. I was in Captivity to Activity. I was in captivity to always moving, being busy, always moving, saying, "YES" to every request, thinking I had to be involved in everything. I thought it was a status thing to be busy all of the time and say I was involved in 20 organizations or projects at the same time. In moments when I had nothing to do, I was uncomfortable.

When I was grieving my nephew, or not grieving, I didn't stop, although I was physically tired. During that time, I taught as a full-time professor, taught a 5-week summer graduate course, planned a female conference, tried to help others and tried to push my pain to the side. I didn't stop.

When I move so much, do I even take time to hear from the Lord? Prayer is a conversation—many of us pray and tell Him what we need or want, but I wonder if we truly pause to hear from Him. My friend, breathe and be still.

ACTION:
Take a moment RIGHT NOW to breathe in and out (3 times). Do this while your eyes are closed. Then take a moment to pray and thank God for His blessings. Tell Him what you need. Tell Him you are broken. Tell Him you are hurt. Be still and try to hear from Him.

Take a moment to write out your needs.

_____
_____
_____
_____
_____

For what are you grateful?

_____

_____

_____

_____

_____

On the first day of my new position in West Texas, I recall what happened when my students walked in. They were freaked out. It was their first day of graduate school. They were overwhelmed, and I said, "OK, class, the first thing is 'Breathe.'" They looked at me like I had a horn coming from my forehead. They were overwhelmed.

I wonder what has overwhelmed you right now.

Write it down: Lord I am overwhelmed because . . .

_____

_____

_____

_____

_____

Many of you wear twenty or more different hats. You're a parent, employee, wife, husband, leader of an organization, mentor, daughter, son, volunteer, ministry leader, writer, singer, creator, and more. That's how it's supposed to be, right? Busy all of the time? Some of you reading this book are so lost, hurt, and frustrated that you are trying to keep busy in order to not deal with the pain. But what you might learn is being busy doesn't help in the long run. Trying to bury hurt and pain is not helpful, even though I know that's what we do. Even though, that's what society tells us to do. That's what we are taught. That's what we saw our parents do, right?

Sometimes, you need to fully feel what you are feeling. And know what you feel is OK. But remember that our feelings are not faithful! Remember to ask yourself, "Am I trusting my feelings more than the Lord?"

Have you ever thought or said, "I can't be still; I have too much on my plate." But do you need to be still? How does moving 100 miles per hour benefit you and your family? How does it hurt you? Are you trying to move 100 miles per hour but know you are on fumes?

I know what it means to be on fumes, and it isn't good. I pushed myself too much. I tried to do things in my own strength. I didn't seek the Lord. I wasn't still. I was trying to take care of everyone, but me. I forgot that God is in control and is the Ultimate Comforter. I forgot that it was OK to take a break. I forgot that it was OK not to be OK. But we must remember Who is on the throne.

What are you afraid might happen if you stop?

_____

_____

_____

_____

_____

ACTION:
Write down the words to Psalm 46:10 and place it somewhere that would be a good reminder for you—your cell phone, on your mirror, in your car, on your computer.

Now trust me, I understand there will be days when God will carry us, as He did on that day I had that speaking engagement, but it's actually selfish of us not to be still and allow the Lord to replenish us. Remember that sometimes the replenishment is not just for us to go out and pour it out, but maybe it is for us to be replenished fully for a moment.

You might be thinking, "Well I want the best for my kids, and I can't stop." If you are running around ragged, do your kids see you running around ragged? You know, they do learn from you. I never saw my mother or father rest growing up. I remember in 1999 going on a vacation with my mom, sister and brother to Las Vegas. I remember the bulk of that trip was staying by a payphone, while my mother was closing business deals.

She and my father got divorced in 1995, and she wanted to keep the same lifestyle to which we had become accustomed. So what did that mean for her? She worked 20 hours a day. She was exhausted. My mother is the most amazing person I know. Her love is powerful, but I did wish that she would have rested. Unbeknownst to myself and her, that was passed on to me.

How can you relate to this? Do you need to forgive your parent(s) or apologize to your children? This doesn't mean that your parents or you aren't amazing. It just means you are releasing a burden.

_____

_____

_____

_____

_____

In the spring of 2017, I was leading a training session where I was discussing rest and self-care. A gentleman shared that he never saw his father rest, and now, he also doesn't rest. He shared a motto that he follows which is, "I'll sleep, when I'm dead." This is such a dangerous thing to follow. Being still is not a weakness; it is not a bad thing, and the Lord tells us to do it. If we are always moving, is this telling the Lord, "I got it?"

For me, being too busy, being busy, and never stopping was really my way of telling the Lord that I didn't trust Him. And this revelation was an "ouch" moment for me.

Have you ever had surgery? Well you know there are various doctor's orders to recover. After my surgery to remove the tumor, I was told just to take it easy. What might have happened if I went back to normal activity too soon? Pain, prolonged healing, possible injury. There was nothing I could do to rush the healing, except be still.

There are many people walking around who have not emotionally healed. They still have pain because they have not allowed the Lord to heal them.

Is this you? Describe.

_____
_____
_____
_____
_____

What consumes your thoughts?

_____

_____

_____

_____

_____

What thoughts came to mind as you read this chapter?

_____

_____

_____

_____

_____

What does rest look like for you?

_____

_____

_____

_____

_____

As a friend shared with me, "Resting and being stationary are not the same thing." Really take a few moments to sit in that. We often will get sick and say, "Well, I was in bed the whole time." But did you rest? Probably not, because you were worried about tasks.

Finally, please don't say the phrase, "Time heals all wounds." This isn't true. It's what you do with the time—and—some wounds will never fully heal. After my nephew went to be with the Lord, I now say that I have learned to live life with a limp. And that is OK.

QUESTION
Take a moment and read Luke 10:38-42.
What was Mary doing?

_____

_____

_____

_____

_____

What was Martha doing?

_____

_____

_____

_____

_____

Who did Jesus say was doing the right thing? And why?

_____

_____

_____

_____

_____

Who can you relate to? Mary or Martha?

_____

_____

_____

_____

_____

ACTION:
CREATE YOUR 'BE STILL' PLAN

Why is being still important for you RIGHT NOW in this season?

_____

_____

_____

_____

_____

When and where can you take time each day to be still? (even if just 5 minutes)

_____

_____

_____

_____

_____

Suggestions:

- Visit the water and just sit.

- Turn off your phone for a moment.

- Just lay down.

- Breathe and Pray.

- Put on your favorite praise and worship song.

- As you drive from work—no music or phone.

- Take a nap.

- Take time throughout the day to take deeps breaths in and out.

- Go on a trip to see nature.

- Get a hotel room for the night.

- Say No.

Who can you invite to hold you accountable in being still?

_____
_____
_____
_____
_____

Now, give them a call to ask if they wouldn't mind doing this.

Write your prayer regarding breathing and being still.

_____
_____
_____
_____
_____

One final time: Take a few moments to slowly inhale and exhale a total of three times. Remember to Be Still, Breathe, and Pray.

WALKING THROUGH THE FOG

Chapter 7

STEP 2: PRAY: EVEN IF YOU DON'T KNOW WHAT TO SAY

"Hear my prayer, LORD, listen to my cry for help;
do not be deaf to my weeping. I dwell with you as
a foreigner, a stranger, as all my ancestors were"
(Psalm 39:12).

"The LORD is close to the brokenhearted and saves
those who are crushed in spirit" (Psalm 34:18).

Describe what you need the Lord to do.

_____
_____
_____
_____
_____
_____
_____

I would like to share something author Lysa Terkeurst shared on her Facebook page:

> "Over time, I've learned that God Himself comes to us personally when we're afraid or grieving. Even when we can't process what life throws at us, we can know that God stays with us.
>
> "And He never leaves. No matter how messy our grief gets."

This is how I felt at times. I didn't even know what to ask for or to say. It was hard to process what was going on. But I am thankful that the Lord was there.

Too often, I have not paused to talk to Him because I forgot, I was frustrated, I felt bad that I hadn't spent time with Him in a while, I was broken and more. Guess what? He can handle all of that. Just go to Him. Even if all you say, is, "Lord, Help."

When you are in a place where you are broken, confused, and hurt, prayer is the best method. And when you're in a place where you are not broken, confused, and hurt, prayer is still the best method. I wonder if any of you have ever been in a place where you wanted nothing to do with the Lord. After my nephew passed away, there were some family members who were angry and wanted nothing to do with the Lord.

A good friend of mine shared with me that she told the Lord, "I'm just letting You know, but I'm not talking to You."

She was hurt and broken.

She later heard the Lord say, "Even if you are not talking to Me, I'll still be here."

Although I never said those words, "I'm not talking to You," my actions said them quite often.

Because prayer is so important, I would like to present to you a prayer guide that Tay, one of my lovely mentees, designed.

PRAYER

"WHAT IS IT?

It is dialogue between you and our heavenly Father. In the same way that relationships have no chance at thriving without consistent and purposeful communication, our relationship with Christ will not grow and flourish if communication with Him lacks in purpose and consistency.

"HOW DO I KNOW WHAT TO PRAY FOR?

One of the things that is really great about prayer is the individuality attached. God made you and me very differently, which means that our communication with Him will look different all around. Often, we feel as though there is so much to be in prayer about, so we have a difficult time deciding what we will pray for today and what we will for tomorrow and so on. Here is a list that I go by when I spend my devotional time in prayer with the Lord:

PRAY FOR OTHERS

"This is the time when I spend time praying for as many people as I can: my loved ones, my students from school, my mentees and students in youth ministry, the people that I work with, the people that I do ministry with, strangers and anyone else. One of the things that helps me in this area is splitting up the days.

THANKSGIVING

"This is an opportunity to be thankful to the Lord for any and everything that He has done and has given. Typically, I will put all of my praise reports in this part of the prayer.

REPENT

"This is an opportunity to talk with the Lord about where I am falling short. I will confess my sin for the day, the minute, the hour and so on in this section. The more real and authentic and genuine you are with the Lord about your sin, the more He can come in and change those areas of your life.

MY NEEDS

"This is the time to pray for you. Here is where I share my needs with the Lord. Things that are happening in my life that I do not understand, screaming/crying/yelling happens here and more. At this point in the prayer, it is about you.

"It always helps if there is a model of how to do the things that we do not know how to do. People in the Bible prayed! It sounds different and looks different, but it does give us a picture of what it looks like to pray for all these things or just one of these things. I hope that these passages are helpful and encourage you to pray!!

"David sinned against the Lord by committing adultery. His praying for forgiveness and healing for a broken heart is an example of how authentic it should sound when we pray.

"Hannah could not have children. The prayer she prayed for her son, Samuel, is one of desperation and surrender. She understood that while a son is what she desired, she knew that it had to be on God's terms.

"Job prayed constantly through all of his experiences:

through the good and the bad. This reminds us that it is okay to be real with the Lord about what we are going through and how we feel. Talking with Christ about how your situations affect you is not wrong."

Prior to 2013, I hadn't often prayed. I might do the obligatory meal prayer, but when I would pray, I wouldn't be seeking God's guidance or help. I was essentially telling Him what I wanted, which isn't entirely wrong. I didn't wait for or seek an answer because I had myself on a pedestal. I had quiet time and was learning scripture, but I cannot think of a time when I asked the Lord for help without me already truly having an answer. I am thankful for the quiet time and the scriptures I was learning, as they would come in handy later, having no clue that they would.

For the most part, until 32 years of age, I thought I knew everything, would not ask for help and was offended if someone would give me advice. It was like I was the Lord of my life, and I tried to be the Lord in other people's lives. Honestly, I began talking to the Lord after the break up, and then I truly had no other choice but to seek Him after my nephew passed away. Why does it often have to be something really hard that brings us to the Lord?

When is the last time you said, "Lord, I need you?"

ACTION:
Pause and pray:
Lord, I need you

_____

_____

_____

_____

_____

_____

My prayer life continued to grow after I left my job. I was hearing and seeing the Lord in ways I had never seen Him. It's amazing what just talking to Him, listening to Him and trying to trust Him will do. But I will not pretend that this journey hasn't been scary, confusing and frustrating.

There have been times I have felt so lost, confused, devastated and bitter that I felt like I couldn't pray, and I am thankful others were praying for me. This might be you. All you have to do is tell the Lord, "Help me. Please meet me right where I am." I want to encourage you to ask a few people to pray for you. Just say, "Pray for me!"

We often feel like we have to apologize for our reaction to life happenings, or we have to fit in this perfect grief box. Your experience is your experience. You don't have to convince people to believe it. You don't have to feel bad for it.

There is a phrase that is overused when going through hard times, and it doesn't help. The phrase is, "You're strong." I sure didn't feel strong, and I bet you don't either. And it's not our strength anyway.

You know that life is messy at times, hard, and devastating. And guess who also knows this, the Lord. So, take all of your mess to Him. It doesn't have to be pretty.

When I was below fumes and went to the lake house—those three days were so messy. I cried, yelled out, repented, asked for help, realizing that I had been holding on to so much. It was messy and beautiful.

So my friend, you don't have to do things on your own. You don't have to hide your pain.

ACTION:
Consider doing what I like to call "Dr. G's 5 Squared method" in your daily or weekly journaling.

Write 5 things for each of the following 5 categories:
- For what are you thankful?
- At what are you good?
- What are your opportunities for growth?
- Prayer Requests.
- Praise Reports.

Before we head to the next chapter, I challenge you to take time to think and answer the following questions.

How have you seen the Lord during this time?

_____

_____

_____

_____

_____

WALKING THROUGH THE FOG

How has the Lord provided for you?

_____

_____

_____

_____

_____

How have you made it this far?

_____

_____

_____

_____

_____

What are a few 'go to' scriptures you use for prayer?

_____

_____

_____

_____

_____

Please don't forget to PAUSE . . .
- Pray
- Always
- Using
- Scripture for
- Everything

STEP 2: PRAY: EVEN IF YOU DON'T KNOW WHAT TO SAY

PLAN FOR PRAYER:
When can you make time to pray?

_____
_____
_____
_____
_____

What do you need to pray? (Journal, Bible, etc.)

_____
_____
_____
_____
_____

How can you be more intentional about incorporating prayer into your life?

_____
_____
_____
_____
_____

Is there someone you know who is going through a hard time? How can you pray for them?

_____
_____
_____
_____
_____

Some ways to remember to pray:
- Praise and worship songs
- When you see the color green, say a prayer.
- When you wake up say, "Good morning, Jesus."
- Be intentional; don't just thrown prayer on the back burner.
- Arrive 10 minutes early, so you can sit in your car and pray.

What's your plan for prayer?

_____

_____

_____

_____

_____

Invite someone on this prayer journey. I challenge you to pray scriptures. I recommend the book *Praying God's Word* by Beth Moore. Here are a few of her prayers:

"Show me Your ways, O Lord, teach me Your paths; guide me in Your truth and teach me, for You are God my Savior, and my hope is in You all day long." (Psalm 25:4-5). "Teach me Your way, O Lord, and I will walk in Your truth; give me an undivided heart, that may fear Your name" (Psalm 86:11). "Mighty God, help me to understand that I've been called by You to walk by faith and not by sight" (2 Corinthians 5:7). Strengthen my spiritual vision, Lord!"

"Dear Heavenly Father: Lord, without You I would be foolish, disobedient, deceived, and enslaved by all kinds of passions and pleasures. I would live in malice and envy, being hated and hating others" (Titus 3:3). I don't want that kind of life, God! I want to live life in the power and fullness of Your Spirit.

"Dear Heavenly Father: Lord, according to Your Word, what a man desires or craves deeply is unfailing love" (Proverbs 19:22). Every other use of the words unfailing love in Scripture is attributed to You alone. You are the only one capable of perpetually unfailing love. Help me to understand that my deep cravings for someone to love me with that kind of love were meant to be satisfied in You alone. Thank You, Lord.

"Dear Heavenly Father: I praise You, Lord, with all my soul, and I desire never to forget all Your benefits—You, Lord, are the one who forgives all my sins and heals my diseases, who redeems my life from the pit and crowns me with love and compassion, who satisfies my desires with good things so that my youth is renewed like the eagle's. You, Lord, work righteousness and justice for all the oppressed" (Psalm 103:2–6).

Your Turn. Just Pray

_____

_____

_____

_____

_____

WALKING THROUGH THE FOG

Chapter 8

STEP 3: BE HONEST
"IT'S OK NOT TO BE OK"

"In my distress I called to the LORD; I cried to my God for help. From his temple he heard my voice; my cry came before him, into his ears" (Psalm 18:6).

Describe the last time you cried out to the Lord.

_____
_____
_____
_____
_____

How often are you honest with the Lord?

_____
_____
_____
_____
_____

During a consultation with a potential client, she revealed to me that she had been violated by someone at work. One of the questions I asked her, based on her tone was,

"Are you angry?"

She said, "I'm not supposed to be angry."

I then asked, "But are you?"

She again said, "I am not supposed to be angry."

I asked again, "But are you?"

She said, "Yes."

I asked her, "Have you admitted that to anyone?"

She said, "No."

We were then able to continue the conversation and begin the work.

I was having a conversation with a family member who had an anger problem. I asked him what he does with his anger, and he shared that he releases it at the gym or he might yell at a co-worker. I later asked him if he knew why he was so angry.

He then said, "I think my dad could have done more for my family."

I said, "Do you think you have the right to be angry about this?"

He said, "Yes."

I responded, "You do. But you can't live there." I then said, "Have you ever admitted this to anyone including the Lord."

He said, "No."

So for over 20 years he had pent-up anger and never told anyone or began to do anything about it. We then began the process of surrendering and admitting these thoughts and feelings to the Lord.

For me, six months after I left my professor position, I received the largest contract I had gotten to that date. I was so grateful. To my surprise, that large contract was taken away. I never admitted to anyone how hurt and bitter I was. It hit me one day that I was carrying this around and had to forgive the organization and ask the Lord for help. Also during the time after leaving the professor position, I thought I made a mistake and told the Lord that. I struggled emotionally and financially during that time and it was hard. There were times I cried out to the Lord saying "Lord, did I make a mistake?" "Lord, what is going on?" But each time I thought I was making a mistake, I remembered the peace I had when I was obedient in leaving the job. I had to remember the tree tops analogy to help me through. I had to focus on the Lord and not my circumstances.

Weight, weight loss and a specific size had been idols for me for 20 years. I never admitted to self, others or the Lord how consumed I was by this. I truly never knew how much it was impacting me until the Lord used a sermon in the summer of 2015 to convict me. I immediately began the journey of surrendering these strongholds to the Lord.

Finally, after my nephew passed, I really didn't admit to anyone how hurt I was. I kept it hidden because I wanted to be the helper, but I was broken. It wasn't until that 4-day lake retreat that I was truly honest.

I wonder how many of you are carrying around hurts that can potentially hurt you or even others. I wonder how your hurt has already harmed you. I wonder how many of you are lying to yourselves about your pain.

QUESTION:

What bitterness, unforgiveness, anger, and disappointment are you carrying?

_____

_____

_____
_____
_____

First of all, you need to acknowledge that this is how you feel and this is your truth. But remember that feelings aren't faithful. It's OK to be upset. But you shouldn't hold on to it for too long because it could hurt you. Tell the Lord you are hurt, angry, feel rejected, sad, or heart-broken. Tell Him you need Him.

> "Cast your cares on the LORD and he will sustain
> you; he will never let the righteous be shaken"
> (Psalm 55:22).

Now say this Scripture, but replace 'your' with 'my' and 'you' with 'me.'

"I cast my cares on the LORD, and He will sustain me; He will never let (me) the righteous be shaken."

> "Cast all your anxiety on Him because He cares
> for you" (1 Peter 5:7)

Now, let's make this first person as if you are talking to the Lord.

"I cast all of my anxiety on You, Lord, because You care for me."

What anxieties and cares do you need to give to the Lord?

_____

_____

_____

_____

_____

Your shoulders are not big enough to carry all of your burdens and the burden of others. Pray about this and ask the Lord to help you. Surrender these things to the Lord. Ask Him to replace these burdens with His grace, comfort, peace, love, joy, etc.

As I previously shared, I had emergency surgery on December 17, 2016, to remove a tumor that was twisting one of my ovaries. Until that day, I had no clue that I had a tumor growing in me, but once I felt that pain, it soon became unbearable. In order to remove it, surgery had to happen. I then had to heal from the surgery, which was painful, but necessary. After the surgery, the Lord connected the experience to how we carry around things that can hurt us.

We are carrying around hurt and pain that we may not even realize is there until it hurts us or someone else. We have a choice—we can get rid of it by spiritual surgery—admitting to the Lord, and surrendering it to Him and allowing the Lord to heal us, or we can keep it by pretending like the pain isn't there. Also, there is no time limit on pain. Some pain may last for a long time. But please be encouraged that the Lord is with you in the pain.

Take some time RIGHT NOW to pray and be honest with the Lord.

About what do you need to be honest with the Lord?

_____

_____

_____

_____

_____

What is in you that might be causing some pain?

_____

_____

_____

_____

_____

The day I surrendered my weight stronghold was in the summer of 2015. While watching a sermon online I was led to lie on the floor to pray (I don't ever do this). I started crying and began yelling out, "I don't want this anymore! Lord, I don't want weight to consume me!"

What don't you want anymore?

_____

_____

_____

_____

_____

What are you doing on your own, pretending like you're OK, but you're not?

_____

_____

_____

_____

_____

Very often the response to the question, "How are you doing?" is, "I'm fine," or "I'm good." Many times, that is NOT how we are really doing. In our society we are told to keep moving. Some think it is a sign of weakness to be sad and to ask for help. We are told to power through. We are told not to be mad. We're holding on to stuff that is not ours to handle.

Psalm 131 says, "My heart is not proud, Lord, my eyes are not haughty, I do not concern myself with great matters or things too wonderful for me. But I have calmed and quieted myself, I am like a weaned child with its mother, like a weaned child I am content. Israel, put your hope in the Lord both now and forevermore."

Be honest. My friend, is there anything that you need to release?

Be honest with yourself and God. That's an awesome step to your way to freedom and victory in Christ.

With whom do you need to be honest? A friend, family member? Be sure to pray before sharing as we don't necessarily have to take every wrong someone has done to us to that person. We can forgive and extend grace. Do you need to confess something to a friend or family member?

You know, it's OK to ask for help. It means you are strong enough to acknowledge that you need help.

A pastor once shared with his congregation that he was depressed. He went to counseling and said, "I don't get why I'm depressed because I'm in my Word every day."

The counselor said, "You're in your Word for your

members, not for you."

So, for those of you who are the helpers, and the strong ones in your family, STOP, BREATHE, and BE HONEST.

- You are tired.
- You don't want to always be strong. And honestly you're not that strong, right?
- You want to rest, but don't know how that truly feels
- You don't know what to do if you aren't in control.

I, too, have gone to counseling while experiencing depression.

I had a student in one of my classes say, "Dr. G, so my relationship ended nine months ago, and we were together seven years, but I'm good; but I'm good, but I'm good."

I asked, "But are you really?"

She said, "No."

We tend to sweep things under the rug or put a time limit on being hurt. Remember, it is not 'time' that heals wounds. It is what you do with that time, and some wounds may never fully heal. You just learn to live life with a limp.

ACTION:

PAUSE and Go to Him now.

Lord, I don't know where to start, but I need to be honest with you about ...

_____

_____

_____

_____

_____

Once you have written this, I encourage you to pray and ask the Lord for help. And if led, please share with a trusted brother or sister in Christ to check on you.

Please write down at least two names of people who can pray for and check on you. You Cannot and SHOULD not Do This Alone!

_____

_____

_____

_____

_____

Call or text them NOW and ask them for help. Be specific. Tell them what you need and how often you would like them to check on you. Give them permission to check on you. Ecclesiastes 4:9-10 tells us "Two are better than one, because they have good return for their labor. If because they have a good return for their labor. If either of them falls down, one can help the other up. But pity anyone who falls and has no one to help them up."

Basically, do not do life alone! I know all about that. I have gone through hard things, and no one knew. Later, I would say, "Five months ago I dealt with something, and it wasn't good." In the past, I rarely told my friends and family if I was struggling in the moment. I always tried to handle it on my own or ignore it.

Something that has always encouraged me is the Beatitudes. Hopefully, they will encourage you, too.

Matthew 5:1-12 . . .

"Now when Jesus saw the crowds, he went up on a mountainside and sat down. His disciples came to him, and he began to teach them.

'Blessed are the poor in spirit, for theirs is the kingdom of heaven.

Blessed are those who mourn, for they will be comforted.

Blessed are the meek, for they will inherit the earth.

Blessed are those who hunger and thirst for righteousness, for they will be filled.

Blessed are the merciful, for they will be shown mercy.

Blessed are the pure in heart, for they will see God.

Blessed are the peacemakers, for they will be called children of God.

Blessed are those who are persecuted because of righteousness, for theirs is the kingdom of heaven.

Blessed are you when people insult you, persecute you and falsely say all kinds of evil against you because of me.

Rejoice and be glad, because great is your reward in heaven, for in the same way they persecuted the prophets who were before you.

WALKING THROUGH THE FOG

Chapter 9

STEP 4: TRUST AND BE OBEDIENT

"If you have a willing attitude and obey, then you will again eat the good crops of the land" (Isaiah 1:19).

How much do you need the Lord?

_____
_____
_____
_____
_____

"I wait for the Lord, my soul does wait, and in His word do I hope. My soul waits for the Lord. More than the watchmen for the morning; indeed, more than the watchmen for the morning"
(Psalm 130:1-6).

I once read a quote that said, "Obedience is required, understanding is optional." A pastor once shared, "God is not interested in our opinion. He's interested in our obedience." Has there ever been a time when you knew the Lord wanted you to do something, yet, it didn't make sense, so you didn't do it? I know I have.

But what does it mean to be obedient?

According to blueletterbible.com, *Strong's Exhaustive Bible Concordance,* "Disobedience of the Israelites is said to be the evidence of their unbelief. Faith is of the heart, invisible to men; obedience is of the conduct and may be observed. When a man obeys God, he gives the only possible evidence that in his heart he believes God."

How do obedience and trust go together?

If you trust the Lord, you will be obedient even when it doesn't make sense. And oh boy have I been there! Obedience and trust don't always feel good. I have been confused, regretted decisions, and wanted to turn back. But as previously stated, I tried to remember the peace I had when I was obedient. However, you might not always have peace, you will just know the Lord is guiding your steps. And I am so thankful for those times I was obedient.

After I left my full-time job to pursue the Lord, I realized I kept looking back at that job way too much. I was holding on to it, holding on to what could have been. But the Lord told me to release. It was as if I was holding on to the job with one hand while trying to reach for "the next" with the other hand. But the entire time the Lord needed me to have both of my hands available for "the next." "Jesus replied, 'No one who puts a hand to the plow and looks back is fit for service in the kingdom of God." (Luke 9:62)

"Remember not the former things, nor consider
the things of old. Behold, I am doing a new thing;
now it springs forth, do you not perceive it? I will
make a way in the wilderness and rivers in the
desert"
(Isaiah 43:18–19).

"Brothers, I do not consider myself yet to have
laid hold of it. But one thing I do: Forgetting what
is behind and straining toward what is ahead, I
press on toward the goal to win the prize of God's
heavenly calling in Christ Jesus"
(Philippians 3:13–14).

What are the things at which you continue to look back, when
the Lord said to release and move forward? How has looking
back hindered you?

_____

_____

_____

_____

_____

The popular hip-hop artist Lecrae has a song called
Background. In it, he tells the Lord to take the lead.

To me, this means that he wants to trust the Lord,
wherever he is taken. I have taken the lead too many times,
but when I do, I get in my own way. I need the Lord to take the
lead because my way does not work. When I take the lead, I
am telling the Lord, "I don't trust you." When He tells me to do
something and I don't or hesitate, I am telling the Lord, "I don't

trust you."

As you are walking through the fog, know that God has your hand. The Lord is saying, "Trust Me." The safest place and sometimes the scariest place to be is holding His hand and being close to His bosom. The Lord knows best. Trust Him and be obedient.

Trust that He will comfort you. Trust that He will meet you right where you are.

I am sure you might be thinking or have thought, "Lord, it is hard for me to trust You. Obedience is scary," or "Lord, I am hurt, and it seems like when I trust You, I get hurt."

Remember chapter five. Tell the Lord all of that.

When that new professor position just seemed to drop out of the sky, I didn't understand why this job, why West Texas, why now? Even on the first day of school, I still didn't understand. And just one year later, the Lord was leading me to leave that very job. So I really didn't understand.

The Lord used many things to tell me to listen to Him, from an excerpt of a message playing on the radio in my car, to the tree tops experience I shared in chapter one, to a devotional I read, to the support of friends, and much more.

Again, I didn't understand why I was leaving this awesome job, but I knew I had to go. I worried about what people might think. What's interesting is I was, at times, more concerned about what others would think over what the Lord thinks and told me to do.

The following excerpt of a writing by my awesome friend, Kai, accurately reflects where I've been:

"After enduring years of bitterness, anger and frustration about situations, I finally truly received the revelation that God is Sovereign, and the Lord's

protection and provision takes many shapes and forms. In trusting in God, I'm agreeing to also trust His will, ways, methods and timing. I've had to learn to trust in His character and heart when I didn't understand the hand I was dealt, the circumstance I was in, or the bad consequences from "good" choices I've made.

"Yes, it totally sounds easier than it feels. However, temporary gratification never feels better or provides more than the promises of God. Trust in the truth that God will not withhold any good thing from you (Psalm 84:11).

"Finally, '[when you move in your own strength or choose not to trust the Lord, you give] the impression that you KNOW what's best for you. We ignorantly believe that as one who was created we know more than the One Who created us. I know it's a surprise, my friends, but we do NOT. We are humans capable of free-will (to an extent) and decision-making; however, these are both limited to our human knowledge, experience, wisdom and information. No matter how smart you are, if you do not have all the facts/information, then you cannot make the best decision. We are limited to our own natural ability; whereas, Christ is limitless. When we succeed, it's because He puts His supernatural on our natural. He knows all, sees all, created all and can fix all.

"How can you know where and when you're supposed to be, if you don't know where and when you're supposed to be? I admonish us all instead to concentrate on Whose we are and what Jesus did, instead of what position or status we have."

WALKING THROUGH THE FOG

My friend, how do you relate to Kai?

_____

_____

_____

_____

_____

Why is it important for you to trust God?

_____

_____

_____

_____

_____

Do you believe the Lord wants you to slow down, grieve, take a leap of faith, forgive, know it's ok not to be ok? So what keeps you from trusting Him and doing so?

_____

_____

_____

_____

_____

Since 2013, I have been on a journey of obedience, or trying to be obedient. Most of the things I've done I would have never thought I would do, but I felt a nudge from the Lord.

Here's one of my first bouts with obedience, and I had no clue why I was doing this. A month before I began the new professor position in 2013, a woman called me while I was in the store and said, "Dr. G, I've been looking at your card for the past couple of hours, and God told me to call you." I didn't know this woman. Long story short, she told me she was looking for opportunities to work and needed some help. I said, "Umm, call me back at 8:45." I didn't know what I was going to tell her. I just said call me back.

During that time God said, "You're going to meet with her and help her."

"Umm, excuse me? I have my schedule already laid out for Saturday. I'm doing this at 9:00; I'm going to box at 11:00; I'm meeting with my thesis student at 1:00. Lord, this doesn't really fit."

The Lord said "Go." So she called me back at 8:45 on the dot, and I said, "I don't do this, really ever, with people I don't know at all, but meet me tomorrow at this place." After we hung up, I thought, "Okay cool; so I'm going to meet with her for 30 minutes, and I'm going to get back to my meetings."

Well, we met for two and a half hours. This person began to share that she has nine children, she's homeless, and she's been abused. She's not asking me for money. She's asking for an opportunity to work. God, however, said, "Give."

Money is not my ministry, as I often say in a joking manner. Now, we can talk. We can have a conversation, but He said, "Give!"

I then thought, "Well Lord, You know I have to save money.

He said, "Go." So I went and got the money. In checking my balance, I discovered that there was literally two times more in my account than what I expected. There was a check I got from something that I wasn't expecting. I was like, "Oh, my gosh! Really?" I gave her a bit more money. I am glad that I was obedient.

In May of 2017, I went on an awesome solo road trip to

Branson, Missouri, for my birthday. Per the recommendation of someone who lives there, I went to a restaurant for an early dinner one evening.

The waitress asked me if I was from the area, and I responded that I was not. I told her I was in town for my birthday, and I wanted to be by the water.

She said, "Happy birthday, but I do not like water." I asked her why she didn't and she shared with me that the area had recently experienced a horrendous flood. I then asked her if she had lost anything in the flood. She let me know that her entire apartment was flooded. She also let me know that she was essentially homeless. The Salvation Army was putting her and her husband up in a hotel. She shared how stressed she was. In the midst of sharing, she began to cry. She apologized for the tears and said that she had been trying to focus on other things rather than that. She mentioned that she still trusts the Lord, but things were just hard.

She shared with me that her husband had lost thousands of dollars in tools due to the flood. As she was sharing, I felt the Lord pushing me to give her a hug.

I said, "I know this may be weird but can I give you a hug?" She said, "Yes," and we embraced for about 15 seconds. While we were hugging I prayed for her.

When we released from the embrace she had a smile on her face and thanked me. She walked away.

I then felt the Lord nudging me to do something else to help her. I did that too.

Now, I didn't go on this trip to help anyone. I knew I just wanted to relax. What I learned is we truly cannot shut off our God-given gifts and cannot shut off the Lord. Yes, I wanted to go on a vacation, but I can't go on a vacation from who the Lord has created me to be.

There have been a few times in the past where I knew the Lord was guiding me to do something, and due to various reasons, I was disobedient and did not move or in some cases get still. In that instance in this restaurant, I had no hesitation, and did not care about what anybody might think. My focus was solely on what the Lord was telling me to do.

Also, I almost didn't even go to the restaurant because it didn't look as nice on the outside as I would have liked, but I felt led to go in.

What is the last thing you felt led to do, and you didn't understand why? What was the outcome?

_____

_____

_____

_____

_____

When you choose not to be obedient, what does that look and feel like?

_____

_____

_____

_____

_____

Why is it difficult for you to be obedient to the Lord?

_____
_____
_____
_____
_____

Is there something you know you should do, but you haven't done it yet? What is it?

_____
_____
_____
_____
_____

Why don't you do it?

_____
_____
_____
_____
_____

What prevents you from taking that step in obedience? (It could be a step to leave a job, relationship, start a job, go to counseling, take some time off...)

_____
_____
_____
_____
_____

On a scale 1-10 (1 is no trust, 10 is total trust), how much do you trust the Lord? Be honest.

_____

_____

_____

_____

_____

Now, what do you think needs to happen to get you to the next number? So if you selected 4, what needs to happen to get to a 5?

_____

_____

_____

_____

_____

If your number is low, that's ok. Matthew 17:20 says, "*He replied, 'Because you have so little faith. Truly I tell you, if you have faith as small as a mustard seed, you can say to this mountain, 'Move from here to there,' and it will move. Nothing will be impossible for you.'*"

Do you know that a mustard seed is smaller than a grain of rice? If you have mustard seed faith, the Lord is able to do great things through you.

If you selected 1, thank you for being honest, and the great thing is that I don't think that you would be reading this book if you didn't want the Lord's help.

What is the Lord telling you to do in this season? Be still, forgive, apologize, take that step, leave a job, stay in the job?

_____

_____

_____

_____

_____

I still struggle with being obedient and trusting. I have learned that when I truly let go and trust the Lord and His Word, there is an unexplainable peace.

If I were to encourage you to read any book of the Bible, I would encourage you to begin with Ephesians. This book tells you, who you are in Christ. In the first three chapters, the Apostle Paul tells us what believers have because of being in Christ, and in the final two chapters, Paul gives instructions for what believers should do.

I have one final obedience story to share with you that still amazes me.

Have you ever written letters of apology to people who wronged you? No? Well, I have. This definitely was an act of obedience.

In August of 2013, I attended a church service with a friend. The message was coming to a close. I began to gather my things, and I then heard the pastor say, "If there is any relationship that needs reconciliation, you should address it." A few moments later, three names dropped into my spirit. As much as I tried to ignore this, I couldn't. What I didn't understand was that God was leading me to apologize to some people who I felt had wronged me. I remember thinking, "Umm, excuse me, but she did me dirty, Lord."

I needed to be obedient, so I typed up the first letter. That was easier than the other two because I did believe that I had something for which I should apologize. Once I finished with the email, I attempted to save it in drafts so I could then head to my boxing class, but I physically could not move from the couch. It was as if the Lord was saying, "Send now!" So I sent the first letter of apology. Then, I sent the second one.

This second one was a bit harder. It was to someone I had been friends with for over 20 years. I felt that she misjudged me based on five words. I was hurt. I thought, "We have 20 years, and this is how you treat me?" This one was difficult. Nevertheless, the Lord revealed to me for what I needed to apologize.

The final letter was the hardest. I did not know why He put the person on my heart. We were friends for about seven years, and how the friendship ended caught me by surprise. I was blamed for everything—things that didn't make sense, and things that weren't my fault. I felt as though she found "better friends" and just got rid of me. But the Lord revealed to me for what I needed to apologize. And I did.

Sending the letters might have been more about obedience and providing something they needed, rather than for my benefit.

I did hear back from each person who thanked me. Reconciliation doesn't always mean that you're friends again. It just means hurt was addressed.

As I was writing these letters the following scripture came to mind. *"Do nothing out of selfish ambition or vain conceit, rather in humility value others above yourself"* (Philippians 2:3).

What does that verse mean to you?

_____

_____

_____

_____

_____

Who is someone you need to offer an apology?

_____

_____

_____

_____

_____

What I was learning was that even if someone did me wrong, 95 times out of 100, I can still apologize for what I did.

If you believe the Lord wants you to apologize to someone, why don't you do it now?

What's your prayer for trusting and obedience?

_____

_____

_____

_____

_____

Sit and truly think about any area of your life where you know the Lord is leading you in a certain direction.

_____

_____

_____

_____

_____

God is a good God. He is also a God of consequences. See Romans 6:1, 2.

Is the Lord telling you to Be Still, and are you are choosing to
      keep moving?
Is the Lord telling you to Rest?
Is the Lord telling you to leave or stay at a job?
Is the Lord telling you to get out of or in a certain
      relationship?
Is the Lord telling you to take that step of faith?
Is the Lord telling you that it's ok to grieve, yet you ignore?

_____

_____

_____

_____

_____

Read Proverbs 3:5-7.
    "Trust in the Lord with all your heart,
    And lean not on your own understanding;
    In all your ways acknowledge Him,
    And He shall direct your paths.
    Do not be wise in your own eyes;
    Fear the Lord and depart from evil."

WALKING THROUGH THE FOG

Chapter 10

STEP 5: REMEMBER HOPE

"My Hope is Built on Nothing Less"

By Edward Mote

My hope is built on nothing less
Than Jesus' blood and righteousness;
I dare not trust the sweetest frame,
But wholly lean on Jesus' name.
On Christ, the solid Rock, I stand;
All other ground is sinking sand.

When darkness veils His lovely face,
I rest on His unchanging grace;
In every high and stormy gale
My anchor holds within the veil.
On Christ, the solid Rock, I stand;
All other ground is sinking sand.

His oath, His covenant, and blood
Support me in the whelming flood;
When every earthly prop gives way,
He then is all my Hope and Stay.
On Christ, the solid Rock, I stand;
All other ground is sinking sand.

When He shall come with trumpet sound,
Oh, may I then in Him be found,
Clothed in His righteousness alone,
Faultless to stand before the throne!
On Christ, the solid Rock, I stand;
All other ground is sinking sand.

Hymn #370, The Lutheran Hymnal
Text: 1 Timothy 1:1

I'm sure that you have heard or have even sung the above song. Have you ever truly meditated on the words?

What stands out the most to you?

_____

_____

_____

_____

_____

Our hope can be built on nothing other than the Lord. Nothing! We may try, but it doesn't give us what we need.

I know right now it may be hard for you to have hope. But, my friend, try to hold on to hope in the Lord. Too often, we put our hope in a favorite sports team, in a favorite singer, in our favorite restaurant, in a partner, our job, our car, in the advice of another person, and other fleeting things. Have you ever done this? If so, I bet you were disappointed at some point. Our hope has to be in and on the Lord and His promises.

How crazy is it that we have more hope in a GPS than the Lord?

Are you going into God's presence? Or has your hope in the Lord gone away during this season? During times when things are hard and you're not sure what to do, it can be very hard to have hope in the Lord and to be confident in Who He is. Maybe, you feel like putting your hope in the Lord has caused some unwanted outcomes. Maybe, you feel alone, but you are not.

At the end of 2013, I was broken and was hopeful in what the Lord would do through counseling. Really, I had no choice because it had gotten so bad. I was putting my hope in me. After leaving my professor job, I was hopeful that the Lord would not lead me astray, even though there were times I took my eyes off of Him. And even though I did, the Lord never left me or led me astray.

Go to the Lord and tell Him, "I need you." "I am hurt." "Please give me strength, wisdom, guidance." Be confident that He has all you need and that you don't have to do all of the work.

Describe where your hope has been.

_____

_____

_____

_____

_____

What 2 steps can you take today that displays hope in the Lord and nothing or no one else?

_____

_____

_____

_____

_____

After you've done this, text or call that accountability friend and share with them the steps you want to take.

Hold on to hope.

So in whom are we putting our hope?

The following was retrieved from josh.org:

Because God is all-powerful …
He can help me with anything.

"O Sovereign LORD! You have made the heavens and earth by Your great power. Nothing is too hard for You!" (Jeremiah 32:17).

- God has the power to create anything from nothing (Psalm 33:6-9)
- God has power to deliver (Exodus 13:3)
- God's creative power is beyond our comprehension (Job 38:1-11)
- God speaks and things happen (Psalm 29:3-9)
- His resurrection power is immeasurably great (Ephesians 1:19-20)
- His creation reflects His power (Psalm 19:1-4)
- His powerful word sustains everything (Hebrews 1:3)

Because God is ever-present ...
He is always with me.

"Where can I go from Your Spirit? Where can I flee from Your presence? If I go up to the heavens, You are there; if I make my bed in the depths, You are there. If I rise on the wings of the dawn, if I settle on the far side of the sea, even there Your hand will guide me, Your right hand will hold me fast. If I say, 'Surely the darkness will hide me and the light become night around me,' even the darkness will not be dark to You; the night will shine like the day, for darkness is as light to You" (Psalm 139:7-12).

- All creation is dependent upon His presence (Colossians 1:17)
- God's continual presence brings contentment (Hebrews 13:5)
- God is everywhere and no one can escape Him (Psalm 139:7-12)
- No task is too large or too difficult for Him (Jeremiah 32:17, 27)
- One cannot hide from God (Jeremiah 23:23-24)

Because God knows everything ...
I will go to Him with all my questions and concerns.

"He determines the course of world events; He removes kings and sets others on the throne. He gives wisdom to the wise and knowledge to the scholars" (Daniel 2:21)

Because God is sovereign ...
I will joyfully submit to His will.

"All the people of the earth are nothing compared to Him. He has the power to do as He pleases among the angels of heaven and with those who live on earth. No one can stop Him or challenge Him, saying, 'What do You mean by doing these things?'" (Daniel 4:35).

- God controls time and seasons (Daniel 2:21)
- God has dominion over the affairs of people (Job 12:13-25)
- God chose His people to become like Christ (Romans 8:28-30)
- God chose His people before He made the world (Ephesians 1:4)
- God's eternal purpose is to make His wisdom known (Ephesians 3:10-11)
- He raises and removes rulers (Daniel 2:21)
- He has a plan for His people and will carry it out (Ephesians 1:5, 11)
- He is the only Sovereign (1 Timothy 1:17; 6:15)
- Relationship with God requires worship (John 4:24) (josh.org)

From this information, what resonated with you the most?

_____

_____

_____

_____

_____

Select a few of the attributes of God that are listed above. Write them down somewhere so you can be reminded of "In Whom to put your trust."

WALKING THROUGH THE FOG

Chapter 11

STEP 6: BE GRATEFUL

"Give thanks to the LORD, for he is good;
his love endures forever" (1 Chronicles
16:34).

"Give thanks in all circumstances; for this is God's will
for you in Christ Jesus" (1 Thessalonians 5:18).

"Let the peace of Christ rule in your hearts, since as
members of one body you were called to peace. And
be thankful" (Colossians 3:15).

First Thessalonians says to be thankful in all circumstances. Well quite frankly, this was quite impossible for me at times. And I know it may be difficult for you to be grateful during this time. Being grateful doesn't negate the fact that some hard things are going on. Being grateful allows us to remember that even in the midst of difficult times, we have something for which to be grateful.

List 5 things for which you are grateful:

_____

_____

_____

_____

_____

That might have been difficult for you to do. When things are hard, it can be challenging to find things for which you are grateful.

The following are times that were difficult for me to be grateful.

1. When my nephew went to be with the Lord. I did eventually find gratefulness. I was grateful that I am his aunt. I was grateful for how the Lord kept my sister, brother-in-law and older nephew. I was thankful for the prayers, but I was also in pain. I was thankful that the Lord was with me during the pain.

2. After I left my professor job, during some hard moments, it was hard to be grateful because I was struggling financially. I thought I made a mistake. But then I realized how blessed I was to have a home, a car, family and more. I do wish that I would have focused on this more than what I saw. I spent too much time living in regret, looking back at what I had, and focused on money. While the amount in my bank account decreased and scared me, I still had a bank account.

3. After I gained weight. As I mentioned earlier, there was a time when I made weight into an idol. After I gained weight, I allowed how I felt to negatively impact my mood and how I saw myself, which impacted how

I treated others. One thing that helped me change my perspective was something I read in a magazine that pertained to wanting to lose weight. It said, "in comparison to the more serious challenges faced by other people, I'll take this one." This brought some perspective. Now, I try to remember to be grateful for a body that can move, my health, and the ability to lose weight, should I so choose to do so.

During some of my darkest times, a song called *Dear God* by gospel artist Smokie Norful helped me. The words are:
"It feels so good to make it this far,
And I didn't think I could take it so long,
There were days I wanted to quit,
I said 'surely this is it,'
But I held on,
And I watched as so called friends turned and walked away,
It hurt so much I didn't have words to say,
But even when my day turns to night,
And nothing seems just right,
Lord, I thank You for my life.
Lord, I thank You for every victory,
All the moments You kept me,
I thank You."

Take a moment to thank the Lord:

_____
_____
_____
_____
_____

WALKING THROUGH THE FOG

To which parts of the Smokie Norful song can you relate?

_____

_____

_____

_____

_____

How have you gotten this far?

_____

_____

_____

_____

_____

Describe a time you wanted to quit, and you didn't.

_____

_____

_____

_____

_____

Who are some of the people who helped you on this journey?

_____

_____

_____

_____

_____

I challenge you to reach out to them now and thank them for how they have supported you.

In the midst of a storm people will say, "When one door closes, another will open." But are you praising Him in the hallway? Well, are you?

Consider the phrase, "Rejection is sometimes God's protection." Maybe He had to shut that door, and lock it, so you couldn't get in there.

Have you ever felt rejected? I wonder if it was for a greater reason.

I remember getting that large contract in 2015 and then it being taken away. And on top of that, someone who I brought on board wound up getting a bigger contract. I harbored bitterness and jealousy. I felt thrown away. I later realized that one of the reasons for the contract removal was so I would not make anything other than the Lord into an idol.

As fast as God can open a door, He can close it. That was a hard time. However, I am grateful for the lesson, the opportunity and for the opportunity for my colleague. Can you relate? I wish I would have remembered gratefulness a bit more during that time. I was looking through the lens of feeling forgotten. I was hurt. I had to admit my hurt, give it to the Lord, and remember that He never forgot me.

Describe a time you thought you were forgotten, but learned that you weren't.

_____

_____

_____

_____

_____

Is there something you once prayed for and didn't get? Now, looking back, you are thankful that God didn't answer that prayer? Maybe that job, that engagement, that relationship. Describe it.

_____

_____

_____

_____

_____

Thank Him!

_____

_____

_____

_____

_____

Has God protected you?

Has He guided you?

Has He given you food?

What else?

1 Chronicles 16:8 says, *"Oh give thanks to Lord. Call on his name. Make known his doing among the people."* Do we thank Him? It's very easy to thank Him when things are seemingly calm, right?

"I Have To" OR "I Get To"
This is a phrase I am sure you have said many times. But how about this? What if instead of saying, "I have to," you replace it with, "I get to!"

Try it-
I have to go to work.
I have to get gas.
I have to clean up.
I have to pick up my kids.
I have to submit this paper.

Now say,
I get to go to work ... this means you have a job.
I get to get gas ... this means you have a car, money to pay for gas, and somewhere to go.
I get to clean up ... this means you have the ability to move, and something to clean.
I get to pick up my kids ... you have your kids to pick up.
I get to submit this paper ... this means you are in school and are working on a degree or a certification.
This brings us to gratefulness! How awesome!

What are some of your "I Have To's?"

_____
_____
_____
_____
_____

WALKING THROUGH THE FOG

Now change them to "I Get To"

_____
_____
_____
_____
_____

How have you seen the Lord during this season?

_____
_____
_____
_____
_____

Take a moment and write 20 things for which you are grateful

1. _____
2. _____
3. _____
4. _____
5. _____
6. _____
7. _____
8. _____
9. _____
10. _____
11. _____
12. _____
13. _____
14. _____

15. _____
16. _____
17. _____
18. _____
19. _____
20. _____

I bet you could write even more!

_____
_____
_____
_____
_____
_____
_____
_____
_____
_____
_____
_____
_____
_____
_____
_____
_____
_____
_____
_____
_____
_____

WALKING THROUGH THE FOG

_____

_____

_____

_____

_____

_____

_____

_____

_____

_____

Chapter 12

HOLD ON

Hold on. Don't let go. Hold on to the hope that is in the Lord.

I pray that the previous chapters have helped you in some way. I pray that you took the time to truly answer the questions, pray, surrender to the Lord, and take the time you need.

So, what is the next step? To hold on. My friend, you might want to consider reviewing chapters 6-11 again. As I have said, there is no time limit on walking through the fog. It seems that in some way we are always walking through the fog. There are just times when that fog is much thicker than other times. There is no formula that works the same for everyone. The only consistency is the Lord.

Remember that, "God is good. God cannot lie. God is in charge of everything." I want to offer you a few more pieces of encouragement as you continue to walk through the Fog.

- DO NOT GIVE UP
  Do not throw in the towel. Don't forget that God has sustained you, that He has brought you out of hard things before. Maybe not as hard as what you are going through right now, but He can provide all that you need. And if you feel like giving up, talk to the Lord, talk to a trusted brother or sister in Christ, and seek counseling.

- FEEL WHAT YOU FEEL
  And don't apologize for it. Remember you are experiencing something that you've not before. Remember you might be experiencing trauma or even secondary trauma.

  What is secondary trauma? Trauma you might be experiencing based on working with or helping someone else—compassion fatigue. But remember, feelings aren't faithful. So share your feeling with the Lord and ask yourself, "Is this thought the TRUTH or a LIE?"

  As stated before, you do not have to try to get someone to agree with your experience. Own your experience.

- MAKE SURE YOU BATHE YOURSELF IN SCRIPTURE.
  John Piper asked the question, "How are we supposed to fight the enemy, if we don't have the sword?" You need the Word. That's how we fight the enemy. So take time to study the Word. Place some scriptures in various places.

- YOU ARE VALUABLE
  Don't ever underestimate your value through Christ. Need a reminder? Read Ephesians 1.

- YOU ARE NEEDED
  God is so gracious in that He chose us to carry out His plan. I know that this book is not just about me, but being obedient and the Lord using me to support others.

- THE ENEMY LOVES ISOLATION
  Please do not cut yourself off from people. Allow your loved ones to support you. You are not meant to struggle alone.

- YOU DON'T HAVE TO BE SUPERWOMAN OR SUPERMAN ALL OF THE TIME.
  For me being a superwoman, I told the Lord that I didn't need or trust Him. It's ok to say "NO." It's ok not to be perfect because guess what? You aren't.

  At times you may not have the capacity to do what you once did because you are going through a hard time. And that is ok. Do what you can. Don't push it.

- YOU ARE NOT A MISTAKE.
  Enough said.

- IT'S OK TO TAKE A BREAK.

- IT'S OK TO GO TO COUNSELING.
  What I have learned over the last few years is that we are always walking in the fog. Sometimes the fog might be thicker, but I am always in a time where I am not quite sure what the Lord is doing, and I am learning to just surrender and trust.

  My Blogs—PLEASE VISIT KRISTENGUILLORY.COM for some blogs that might be helpful such as:
  - Break Up Tips
  - The more still I am the More I see God move
  - Captivity to Activity

WALKING THROUGH THE FOG

- Remember the SUN IS SHINING, EVEN IF YOU CAN'T SEE IT

- FOR THE HELPER
  So many of you are the helper, the caregiver, that you need to take time to be restored.

SELF-CARE SUGGESTIONS
- Consider making a fun song list.
- If you are walking through a thick fog—be careful of what you watch on TV.
- Try something new.
- Enjoy the outside.
- Put scriptures on your mirror and in your car and quote them.
- Reach out to someone to help or pray for them.
- Support another person.
- Remember "I GET TO" instead of "I HAVE TO."
- Don't rush.
- Sometimes you will just need to stop.

What revelations did you have as you read this book?

_____

_____

_____

_____

_____

_____

_____

What struggle, frustration or sin do you need to confess to the Lord?

_____

_____

_____

_____

_____

_____

_____

My friend, you are not alone. I'm so sorry for the pain you are experiencing. But I am so glad we serve the Ultimate Comforter. Cry, yell out to the Lord. Do what you need to do.

Remember the Lord knows and is with you. Will you let Him guide you?

Here are a few things I do to rest and for my self-care:
- Zumba/Remix Fit- ratchet Zumba :)
- Watch Netflix
- Get to Atlanta as often as I can to see my nephews
- Go outside
- Sleep
- Eat better
- Forgive
- Pray
- Travel
- Sit by water
- Swim

ACTION
TIME TO CREATE YOUR SELF CARE PLAN:

Why do you need self care?

_____
_____
_____
_____
_____
_____

What does it look like when you don't implement self care?

_____
_____
_____
_____
_____
_____

What can you do throughout the day for your own self care?

_____
_____
_____
_____
_____
_____

What's the first step to take in making sure this happens?

_____
_____
_____
_____
_____
_____

What can you do daily for your own self-care?

_____
_____
_____
_____
_____
_____

What's the first step to take in making sure this happens?

_____
_____
_____
_____
_____

What can you do weekly for your own self care?

_____
_____
_____
_____
_____
_____

WALKING THROUGH THE FOG

What's the first step to take in making sure this happens?

_____

_____

_____

_____

_____

_____

What can you do monthly for your own self care?

_____

_____

_____

_____

_____

_____

What's the first step to take in making sure this happens?

_____

_____

_____

_____

_____

_____

Thank you for allowing me to walk this journey with you. You are not alone.

Here is my prayer for you:

"Lord, I thank You for my sister or brother reading this. Lord, I ask that You meet them right now, right where they are. Lord, I ask that You give them what they need. Lord, please remind them that You can handle what they are going through and that they don't have to do this alone. Lord, I ask that You heal broken hearts. Lord, I ask that You be with them and protect them. Lord, in those dark moments, please allow Your light to shine in some way. Lord, please remind them to breathe. I thank You for their life. In Jesus' name. Amen!

ABOUT THE AUTHOR

Dr. Kristen Guillory is a renowned professor, aunt, owner of a consulting firm, founder of many community initiatives and a sought-after speaker and trainer who uses her own life experiences to help bring out the best in others. Using contagious enthusiasm, transparency, and dance, Dr. Guillory has a life passion to challenge you to release what is holding you back so that you can discover all that is in store for you.

A Dallas native, Dr. Guillory discovered her gift to encourage at the age of 14 and knew she always wanted to help others. Since then, she has created over 60 youth and adult programs, graduated with her bachelor's degree from Texas Christian University, where she is currently teaching in the graduate social work program. She also graduated from the University of Texas-Arlington with a master's and doctorate degree. She has taught at four different universities. She has been invited to present her research in Europe, conducted her doctorate research on the school completion and dropout rates among African-American males, has extensive experience in mental health and is a popular speaker, with her most popular topics being:

- Single is Not a Curse but a Blessing,
- Self-Care,
- Communication,
- Overcoming,
- Cultural Humility, and
- Healing from past hurts.

Dr. Guillory has broken many barriers from earning a Ph.D. at 27 years old, being both the only African-American and woman who graduated with a doctorate from her department that year, to teaching her first graduate class at 24 years old to institutions, creating positions just for her and much more! She thought she knew where life would take her, and then 2013 happened!

After experiencing a tragedy in 2013, her life changed and so did her goals. In 2014, she stepped away from an amazing professor's position in faith, and the journey continues as she strives to be a catalyst for Healing, Hope, and Purpose. Dr. Guillory is excited to be launching some exciting things this year, including releasing her first book.
Dr. Guillory is a member of Concord Church in Dallas, Texas, where she serves as a leader in the Singles ministry.

In her spare time, she enjoys comedy, Zumba, dancing and spending time with her family, especially her nephews!

For further information or to request Dr. Guillory to speak at your conference, go to:

Kristenguillory.com